Make
Prayer
Your Lifestyle
And
Soar.

Arlene

Prayer

THE LIFESTYLE

A 30 DAY CHALLENGE TO A BETTER RELATIONSHIP WITH GOD

Arlene Mitchell

2015

Copyright @ 2015

Printed in USA

Photography: Tanisha Walker

In God's Image Photography / Makeup Artistry

Email: info@ingodsimage.net

Graphic Design: Courtney Moore

cnic/INK

TABLE OF CONTENTS

PREFACE

I was delighted when I was asked to write the preface to this book for several reasons; the most important one being, it affords me a chance to honor and praise God for the work He has done through His vessel, my sister, Minister Arlene Mitchell.

This book represents legacy, victory, and ministry. The legacy is the loving and consistent practice of prayer shared in the Reed home by our late mother, Mother Lillian Marie Reed, which was passed on to members of our natural family, as well as many members of our spiritual family.

Minister Mitchell, a visionary in her own right, took this legacy of prayer to a higher level, when she organized it into a ministry known as Prayer and Empowerment. Little did she know, that God would use her losses and illness to power pack her prayers and give her the ultimate victory. Victory over the very circumstances that could have cost her sanity and salvation. Who better to encourage others than one, who by faith in God and enduring so much, could testify to the power of prayer and the victory it brings.

Finally, the ministry birthed out of this legacy and victory, is yet expanding to now include prayer lines, workshops, shut-ins, coaching, speaking, and now writing about prayer.

I invite every believer to read this God inspired book. Its pages will bless you. It focuses on familiar things we encounter in our walk with Christ and sheds light on the weapons that bring victory over them.

Some of the issues include dealing with death, depression, rejection, anger, and forgiveness. The weapons include faith, courage, patience, peace, love and more. Additionally, it is well organized, plainly written, briefly presented, and scripturally supported.

Rev. Dr. Charlotte Reed Peebles,
Chair Board of Christian Education
Vernon Park Church of God
Chicago, IL

FOREWORD

What Minister Arlene, as she is affectionately known, has done is provided the answers to life's most difficult experiences through the utility of prayer. This is a labor of LOVE – Liability, Obedience, Vehement, Expectation! Prayer is **Liability.** It is a vehicle God has granted us by sending his son, Jesus, to die on the cross for our sins. It serves as mutual obligation as a result of accepting Christ into our lives.

Obedience is manifested through prayer. We are not asked to pray in Matthew 6:6, but instead, the scripture opens with "When you pray," assuming that prayer is an expected regimen. Not one time are we being asked to pray, but instead commanded and compelled; or in essence, being obedient.

Prayer requires us to be **Vehement!** The dictionary defines vehement as *'marked with forceful energy, intensely emotional and deeply felt'*. The power behind our prayer is determined by our force – our fuel. We build our reservoir through prayer.

Finally, there is a belief that when we pray, we do so with **Expectation.** We pray because we expect God to move on our behalf.

~ Dr. Stephanie Helms Pickett
Duke University

DEDICATION

I dedicate this book first to God, my heavenly
Father my Healer and my Friend.

To honor the memory of my mother, the late
Mother Lillian Marie Reed, a great prayer
warrior. She left me a spiritual millionaire,
when she imparted to me the value of having a
prayer relationship with God. I will forever be
indebted to her for this rich legacy.

To the best dad in the world Deacon Thomas Reed,
who has become the prayer warrior my mother
always prayed He would be. He now covers us all
in prayer. Dad, I love you to Life!

ACKNOWLEDGEMENTS

To all the people who have prayed, inspired, motivated and encouraged me with their words of wisdom and knowledge throughout my life, I thank you all!

I want to give special thanks to those who have helped me personally to make this project materialize and that is Pastor Barbara Anderson, Denise Coleman, Minister Iva Cunningham, Marilyn Daniels, Dr. Stephanie Helms Pickett, Courtney Moore, Rev. Dr. Charlotte Reed Peebles, Nia Redmond, Jonica Rowland, and Corrine Sledge for sacrificing countless hours of discussions, edits, research, revisions, encouragement, for your wisdom, your guidance, your friendship, your support, sharing your gifts, giving comforting words and your continuous prayers, I appreciate you. Finally, to my coach Karen King, aka *Giggy the Grandmother* for challenging me to complete this book that has been sitting on the back burner for at least 5 years. She planted seeds of encouragement throughout the journey, keeping me accountable to follow it through to the finish. Thank you loads, Karen.

INTRODUCTION

I believe that prayer is our true source of power.
There is nothing more needed than prayer
activated in our lives, in our homes, and in our
nation. To have it in full operation is a requisite for
this day and time.

Through my two bouts with breast cancer,
unsurmountable grief through loss of a child,
husband, church leader and brother, mother,
grandmother, sister, several other brothers, and a
marriage, I can boldly say, that through it all
prayer has been my saving grace. This powerful
weapon, prayer, has been life defining for me and I
want to share it with the world. I'm clear that I
have been kept alive **on** purpose **for** purpose and
that is to revolutionize the world with the power of
prayer.

I want to encourage you to know that there are
unlimited resources in having an intimate
relationship with God. That is the purpose of this
book. I have formulated thirty prayers for you to
pray; one a day. Prayer will not promise you a
trouble-free life but it will provide insight, security,

guidance, peace, and a place of solace in the midst of chaos.

In my journey of life, I've learned that growth requires taking new challenges and going beyond my comfort zone. Well... are you ready to go beyond your comfort zone and take this challenge? Hmmm....did I hear a Yes? Great! – ☺.

The Supplications and Affirmations play a crucial part in this book of prayer. Here is further explanation of both:

THE SUPPLICATION: Supplication is when we come to God in prayer for a variety of reasons.

The Hebrew and Greek words most often translated "supplication" in the Bible mean literally *"a request or petition,"* so a prayer of supplication is asking God for something.

Numerous examples of supplications are found in the Psalms.

For *mercy*, find it in Psalm 4:1

For *leading*, find it in Psalm 5:8

For *deliverance*, find it in Psalm 6:4

For *salvation* from persecution, find it in Psalm 7:1

In the book <u>Too Busy Not to Pray: Slowing Down to Be With God</u>, Bill Hybels and Lavonne Neff share a very easy prayer formula that I find very helpful in trying to establish prayer time in your daily devotion:

"A.C.T.S."

A - Adoration - Worship Him for who He is

C - Confession - Confess your sins

T - Thanksgiving - Be thankful of the many blessings that you have already

S - Supplication - To ask or petition the Lord

I have incorporated an abbreviated version of this formula for each prayer to assist in adapting it to your personal prayer time.

As stated in my chapter on Discipline, (*which you will read later on in the challenge*) my prayer is that after taking this 30 day Prayer Challenge, you would have disciplined yourself to have formulated a habit of spending time in prayer. I'm confident that *__if applied__* you would have developed an appetite for God's presence and PRAYER AS A LIFESTYLE.

THE AFFIRMATION: Affirmations are statements intended to provide encouragement, emotional support, and /or motivation. In our daily affirmations we will be affirming God's word and positive declarations to promote emotional and spiritual empowerment.

Affirming God's word over yourself is essential because it speaks life into our spirit, body and soul. If you take to heart the scriptures, you will understand the importance of speaking out loud the scriptures listed on the pages of this book.

AT THE END OF THE DAY...

YOUR WORDS CREATE YOUR WORLD.

FOOD FOR THOUGHT:

WHAT KIND OF WORLD ARE YOU CREATING?

Ecclesiastes 4:9 shares, *"Two people are better off than one, for they can help each other succeed."*

Encourage someone to take the challenge along with you. Having someone to discuss the challenge with, as well as hold you accountable to reading and praying the word of God daily, will enhance the enjoyment of the journey. ☺

Each page will have a page to write down your application for the day. You may wonder: How do I write an application anyway? An application is your response to God's Word and points you in a *specific direction* and gives you *specific steps* to make the Word alive and transforming.

Here is an acrostic to help you in the process of writing an application: <u>PEACE STEPS</u>. This acrostic represents great application questions – questions that with the grace of God, will lead you to be more like Him every day of your prayer journey and find peace with God and within yourself. After reading your day's scripture and prayer, ask these questions:

Does this scripture and focus word give me a:

Promise to claim?
Example to follow?
Attitude to change?
Command to obey?
Error to avoid?

Sin to confess?
Truth to proclaim?
Exaltation of God or **E**vangelism tip to follow?
Prayer to pray?
Something to thank God for?

For instance, your first focus word is Addiction, with the meditation scripture is 1 Corinthians 10:13. An application statement might look like this:

"Because I claim the promise given in 1 Corinthians 10:13 that God will always be there to help me when I am tempted by addictive desires – when that desire attempts to control me, I will meditate on 1 Corinthians 10:13, remove myself from any person, place or thing that might be causing that desire to rise, and call a faith-filled friend who will prayerfully encourage me."

<u>My personal supplication for this book:</u>

"I pray that my words will convey healing to all the readers and bring transformation to a new life of fulfillment through the power of prayer in Jesus Name I pray – Amen!"

DAY 1

ADDICTION

"Because of Jesus Christ, peace can replace guilt, healthy relationships can be restored, addictions can be overcome."

~ **M. Russell Ballard**

ADDICTION DEFINED: A strong and harmful need to regularly have something *(such as a drug)* or do something *(such as gamble)*; an unusually great interest in something or a need to do or have something.

Do you have a harmful need for something that you know is not good for you? Addiction is a form of slavery. No matter what your addiction, there is help for you. God wants to set you free. His sacrifice on Calvary breaks the yoke of slavery.

Ephesians 3:20 says *"Now to Him Who, by (in consequence of) the [action of His] power that is at work within us, is able to [carry out His purpose and] do superabundantly, far over and above all*

that we [dare] ask or think [infinitely __beyond our__
__*highest prayers, desires, thoughts, hopes, or*__
__*dreams]*__*"*— DO YOU BELIEVE IT? IF SO..... IT'S
A DONE DEAL!

Galatians 5:1
*"Christ has set us free to live a free life. So take your
stand! Never again let anyone put a harness of
slavery on you."*

__My Supplication:__ Lord, You are my Deliverer. In
You I have all that I need. I give You the praise,
glory and honor that are due Your name. I confess
my sins and ask for Your forgiveness. Although I
have repeated the same cycle of addictive behaviors
over and over again, YOU NEVER GAVE UP ON
ME! I thank You, for with Your love I know that I
am destined for greatness. Your love never runs out
and I'm so grateful. Because of You, I have the
privilege to live life in true FREEDOM. This
addiction will no longer be my master. I need Your
assistance and diligence to guide me through this
dark place. Shine Your light on me and deliver me.
This is my prayer, I believe it and I receive it by the
power of Your blood that was shed on Calvary and
by the power of Your name, Jesus – Amen and
Amen!

My Affirmation: I take my stand and do all that is necessary to embrace my new life, free from this addiction. It's not too late. I have God's help. I walk away from those things and people that might stifle my progress to become a whole, healed and better ME.

Meditation Scripture:

1 Corinthians 10:13
"No test or temptation that comes your way is beyond the course of what others have had to face. All you need to remember is that God will never let you down; he'll never let you be pushed past your limit; he'll always be there to help you come through it."

Application for the day:

_____

_____

_____

_____

_____

_____

_____

_____

_____

_____

_____

_____

DAY 2

ANGER

*"Every day we have plenty of opportunities to get **angry**, stressed or offended. But what you're doing when you indulge these negative emotions is giving something outside yourself power over your happiness. You can choose to not let little things upset you."*

~ Joel Osteen

ANGER DEFINED: A strong feeling of being upset or annoyed because of something wrong or bad; the feeling that makes someone want to hurt other people, to shout, etc.; the feeling of being angry.

My mom always taught me never to let the sun go down on your wrath and I hold it dear to my heart even to this day. As I reflect on the untimely death of my husband who died in my arms, I often ask myself what if I was holding on to bitterness in my heart? I never would have had the opportunity to say sorry. What if he left not knowing how much I

23

loved him? It is because of this occurrence I make every effort to live in peace with all men at ALL TIMES. Life is just too short to hold on to anger when we can choose to live in peace and tranquility.

Proverbs 14:29
*"Being slow to get **angry** compares to great understanding as being quick-tempered compares to stupidity."*

My Supplication:
Lord, You are a friend who sticks closer than a brother and I honor Your loyalty. You are gracious and full of compassion. I humbly ask for forgiveness for the sin in my heart. I have drifted away from You and allowed my emotions to get the best of me. I need a personal revival.

In spite of my shortcomings, You have always shown mercy and I thank You so very much. Father, I ask that You create in me a clean heart and renew the right spirit in me. Fill me with great understanding, and allow me to be slow to anger and have a sensitivity to give a soft answer that turns away wrath. I invite You into my interactions and I surrender my will for Yours in Jesus' Name I pray – Amen!

My Affirmation: Today, I will not allow my emotional responses to be filled with anger. I operate in the spirit of self-control. When I feel anger rising, I use discipline and examine my heart.

Meditation Scripture:

Ecclesiastes 7:9
*"Do not be quickly provoked in your spirit, for **anger** resides in the lap of fools."*

Application for the day:

_____

_____

_____

_____

_____

_____

_____

_____

_____

_____

_____

_____

DAY 3

ANXIETY

"Anxiety does not empty tomorrow of its sorrows, but only empties today of its strength."

~ **Charles Spurgeon**

ANXIETY DEFINED: A feeling of worry, nervousness, or unease, typically about an imminent event or something with an uncertain outcome.

Many of us are guilty of living in anxiety, worrying about our bills, kids, relationships, occupations and so much more. This day I want you to make a conscious effort to let go of the *"unfocused thinking"* that has your thoughts wondering and keeps you worrying about your life.

1 Peter 5:7
"Cast the whole of your care [all your anxieties, all your worries, all your concerns, once and for all] on Him, for He cares for you affectionately and cares about you watchfully."

My Supplication: Lord, You are my sanctuary. My place of relief where I can take a break in your loving arms. I adore You, I worship You. Thank You for forgiving me of my sins and reviving my soul again. You are so gracious and I am so thankful. Thank You for the strength to not fret or worry about anything. Instead of worrying, I WILL PRAY.

I will cast all my cares on You for I know You care for me. I will let my petitions and praises shape my worries into prayers. Thank You for being concerned about me and reassuring me of your love. I can stand in faith believing that everything is coming together and working in my favor. I can rest now because of your word. I can rest now because your peace is taking root in my spirit. Thank You for replacing all anxiety with your peace, in Jesus' Name I pray – Amen!

My Affirmation: I do no fret or worry about anything. God cares for me affectionately and cares about me attentively and that makes me feel safe!

Meditation Scripture:

Philippians 4:6-7
"Don't fret or worry. Instead of worrying, pray. Let petitions and praises shape your worries into prayers, letting God know your concerns. Before you know it, a sense of God's wholeness, everything coming together for good, will come and settle you down. It's wonderful what happens when Christ displaces worry at the center of your life."

Application for the day:

_____

_____

_____

_____

_____

_____

_____

_____

_____

_____

_____

_____

DAY 4

CHARACTER

*"Be more concerned with your **character** than your reputation, because your character is what you really are, while your reputation is merely what others think you are."*

~ John Wooden

CHARACTER DEFINED: Godly character is consistently doing the right thing at the right time in the right way for the right reason.

A life governed by love, joy, peace, patience, kindness, goodness, faithfulness, gentleness, and self-control is powerful and full of character. Unbelievers are not nearly as impressed with what we *say* as they are with how we *act*, especially under pressure. Our character is not only exposed by our actions but it's also exposed by our **RE-**actions.

The way we respond to a matter is often the unveiling of what's truly in our hearts. If the word of God is in you, it will guide your decisions and

manifest a Godly life. Peter says a Godly life
"*silences*" our critics. Don't you want to silence the
critics? Keep persevering in doing what is right to
build character. You will be reflecting the character
of your Heavenly Father. ☺

Romans 5:3-5
*"Not only so, but we also glory in our sufferings,
because we know that suffering produces
perseverance; perseverance, **character**; and
character, hope. And hope does not put us to shame,
because God's love has been poured out into our
hearts through the Holy Spirit, who
has been given to us."*

<u>My Supplication:</u> Lord, You are the Way, the
Truth, and the Life. I worship and adore You. I
confess my sins to You and ask for forgiveness.
Thank You for keeping your agreement to be with
me for the long haul. Although I haven't done
everything right your love still holds me like a
security blanket. Thank You for your nonstop care
of me. I'm asking You to teach me how to glorify
You in suffering for I know I can only do this with
your help. I want to be able to produce
perseverance because perseverance produces
character and character, hope. God, You know I
need all three. Thank you for the grace to stay
away from communication and associations that
will corrupt good manners. Send those persons
that will promote right living and a Godly

character. As I take the steps to walk in your footsteps, I know Your word will be that flashlight to guide me on the path to righteous living in You, in Jesus' Name I pray – Amen!

My Affirmation: I am equipped for every good work God has planned for me. I exercise character with determination to do the right thing at all times even when no one is looking.

Meditation Scripture:

1 Corinthians 15:33
"Do not be so deceived and misled! Evil companionships (communion, associations) corrupt and deprave good manners and morals and
character."

Application for the day:

_____

_____

_____

_____

_____

_____

_____

_____

_____

_____

_____

_____

DAY 5

COMMITMENT

"Every major accomplishment in a man's life requires a major level of commitment."

~ Jim George

COMMITMENT DEFINED: The act of committing or pledging; an obligation, promise, etc. that restricts one's freedom of action.

Commitment is such a big word. Have you ever been afraid of a word? I was. In my thoughts, I would say, *"what if I commit to this and it fails?"* Have you ever been there? Afraid of failing? Well....I did the Joyce Meyer thing, which is **"I did it afraid"**☺

Writing this book was totally done by the grace of God. It took a whole lot of determination and commitment and I'm so glad I finished what I started. We all need to take challenges in life that stretch our faith. Producing this prayer challenge has stretched my faith in ways I never imagined.

Wow! I'm singing AWESOME in three part harmony! – Lol

I'm smiling real big now because I have faced my fear once again and lived out my commitment to finish what I start. My sisters (Charlotte & Barbara) and I had a cute chuckle when I shared with them saying: *"Now I can relate to you staying up all night to get the project done."* Commitment boils down to love, in my eyes. You know why? Love is an action word; so is commitment. ***If you say you love Christ, then prove it by making a commitment to obey His word.***

Psalm 37:5
"Commit your way to the LORD, trust also in Him, and He shall bring it to pass".

My Supplication: Oh Lord, my Lord, how majestic is Your name in all the Earth! It is to You I submit heartfelt worship and praise. I confess, I have sinned and come short of Your glory. Please forgive me. My heart thanks You for Your commitment to love me through it all. As I learn more about Your character, I fall in love with You all over again. I ask that You teach me commitment to serve You. Help me to rise early to seek You. You will hear my voice morning, noon and night. Not out of a religious obligation, but solely because of who You are to me. Grant me the commitment necessary to walk upright before You. Commitment to share my faith, commitment to love, honor, serve, and give ***generously***. Even when it hurts. I want to be mature enough in You that I don't waver in my faith and shut down when hard times arise. Yes, Father, I want to please You in all that I do. I want to be more like You. You are the Potter and I am the clay, shape me and mold me after Your will. I don't want to be afraid of this word anymore. I want to be able to make a commitment to You and be faithful to it. Please release me from laziness and procrastination. I speak commitment out of my mouth in faith' and I trust You for the strength to follow through with each commitment made to You and to others in Jesus' Name I pray - Amen!

My Affirmation: I will no longer be intimated by the word COMMITMENT. I am in a committed relationship with God. I pledge and take action on developing a healthy lifestyle of communication with the Father daily.

Meditation Scripture:

Psalm 84:12
*"O Lord of hosts, blessed (happy, fortunate, to be envied) is the man who trusts in You [leaning and believing on You, **committing** all and confidently looking to You, and that without fear or misgiving]!"*

Application for the day:

_____

_____

_____

_____

_____

_____

_____

_____

_____

_____

_____

_____

DAY 6

CONFIDENCE

"Confidence.... thrives on honesty, on honor, on the sacredness of obligation, on faithful protection and on unselfish performance.
Without them it cannot live."

~ **Franklin D Roosevelt**

CONFIDENCE DEFINED: A trusting or reliance; an assurance of mind or firm belief in the integrity, stability or veracity of another, or in the truth and reality of a fact.

It's taken some time for me to get to this place but I rejoice that I have confidence in God in all things. Through my personal experiences I've learned that it is better to put confidence in God than in man. I have trust, assurance and a firm belief that the God I serve is a strong foundation on which to stand. He's true to His word, He loves me unconditionally, His mercy endures forever and His compassion never fails. Now that makes me full of CONFIDENCE.

Proverbs 3:26
*"For the Lord shall be your **confidence**, firm and strong, and shall keep your foot from being caught [in a trap or some hidden danger]."*

<u>My Supplication:</u> Lord, You are My God, You are the health of my countenance. I worship You for being the lifter of my head. Please forgive me of my sins and revive my soul once again. I thank You for giving me the courage to believe in who You have made me. Someone who's unique and wonderfully made. You are my confidence, a confidence that is firm and strong and that keeps me from hidden danger.

Thank You Father, for with Your help I have the confidence to conquer any army. I can leap over every obstacle, I can face unsurmountable odds. Because of Your help, I have the confidence to triumph over low self-esteem and depression. I feel completely secure in Your large arms of protection while You guide me to victory. You are the source of my strength and because of Your sufficient grace for me, I am moving onward in Your confidence. Because of my awareness in You I will no longer walk in fear and intimidation in Jesus' Name I pray – Amen!

My Affirmation: I have confidence that God has started something wonderful in my life and I have confidence He will never give up on me. He completes His work in me, and brings it to full fruition.

Meditation Scripture:

Proverbs 14:26
"In the fear of the LORD there is strong confidence, and his children will have refuge."

Application for the day:

_____

_____

_____

_____

_____

_____

_____

_____

_____

_____

_____

DAY 7

COURAGE

"Courage is grace under pressure."

~ **Ernest Hemingway**

COURAGE DEFINED: The quality of mind or spirit that enables a person to face difficulty, danger, pain, etc., without fear; bravery.

Courage is required to step out of your comfort zone and do things differently. Sometimes, conquering the unknown while feeling afraid and trusting God to see you through are the best ways to weather the storms of life. Courage is persevering in the face of adversity. No matter what, KEEP MOVING FORWARD! Some may ask, "How can I do that?" It's simple; I would advise you to take everything to God in prayer. He is sure to steer you in the right direction and give you the courage to stand tall.

Deuteronomy 31:6
*"Be strong. **Take courage.** Don't be intimidated. Don't give them a second thought because GOD, your God, is striding ahead of you. He's right there with you. He won't let you down; He won't leave you."*

My Supplication: Father, You are my strong tower and my strength I take courage in You. As long as I live I will worship You. I confess my sins and ask for forgiveness. I thank You for redeeming me out of the hand of the enemy. I ask that You rescue me from the sea of intimidation, fear and doubt. Shift me from being a person who walks timidly to someone who walks in strength, courageously.

Father, I appreciate You for always marching ahead of me and paving the way for victory. I need to be courageous and persevere in difficult times. Teach me the significance of dedicating my life to fasting and prayer so I can build up my spiritual muscles. I desire for each day I live, be steps towards shining in the light of You, *courageously* in Jesus' Name I pray – Amen!

My Affirmation: I am strong and courageous. God has girded me with strength for any encounter I will have to face today. I am not intimidated, I am brave, bold, beautiful and ready to impact the lives I come in contact with today.

Meditation Scripture:

Deuteronomy 31:7b
*"Be strong and of good **courage**, for you must go with this people to the land which the Lord has sworn to their fathers to give them, and You shall cause them to inherit it."*

Application for the day:

_____

_____

_____

_____

_____

_____

_____

_____

_____

_____

_____

_____

DAY 8

DEATH

"Let your hope of heaven master your fear of death."

~ **William Gurnall**

DEATH DEFINED: The act of dying; the end of life; the total and permanent cessation of all the vital functions of an organism.

God says in his word that it is appointed for men to live and die, but no matter when it happens, it seems to knock us off of our feet. Ephesians 3:20 shares that God is able to do exceedingly abundantly above all that you can think or ask ACCORDING TO THE POWER THAT WORKS WITHIN YOU.

Even in death, you have the power within you to get through the heartbreak of losing a loved one. I'm a witness that by understanding God's love and sovereignty (*His dominance and control*), you will be better able to persevere through it. It is not God's will for you to get stuck in depression. Press beyond the tears and disappointment and adapt a lifestyle of conversing with God. Speaking His words of comfort out loud during these times will bring healing to your soul.

Psalm 119:28
"My life dissolves and weeps itself away for heaviness; raise me up and strengthen me according to [the promises of] Your word."

<u>My Supplication</u>: Father, My Sovereign God, I worship You in all of Your strength and authority. I confess my sins and ask for forgiveness. I thank You for Your love that ministers to every broken piece of my heart. Without You, where would I be? Admiration is always due to Your name.

My life seems to be drowning in the sea of sadness. In the morning, in the afternoon and late night, I just can't stop the tears from falling. My heart is so heavy. Father, You are the God of all comfort, the only one that can heal me everywhere I hurt. Help! How can I move on? Father – I ASK YOU, HELP ME, PLEASE!! You said in Your word that You would hear the cry of the brokenhearted and heal their wounds. I need You now, Lord, I need You now. You promised not to leave me comfortless. Come now, Father, come now and rescue me. I'm putting my faith in Your words.

You said blessed are they that mourn for they shall be comforted,

Lord - do it!

You said You would comfort my heart and establish me in every good word and work,

Lord -do it!

You said in the multitude of my thoughts You would delight my soul, **Lord do it!** LORD, DO IT FOR ME, RIGHT NOW. I'M DEPENDING ON YOU TO HONOR YOUR WORD in Jesus' Name I pray – Amen!

My Affirmation: Today, I am no longer governed by my emotions, but I am governed by God's words. Nothing missing and nothing broken, God's comfort and strength are mine. I am getting through this. My better and lighter days are ahead of me.

Meditation Scripture:

2 Thessalonians 2:16-17
"Now may our Lord Jesus Christ Himself and God our Father, who has loved us and given us eternal comfort and good hope by grace, comfort and strengthen your hearts in every good work and word."

Application for the day:

_____

_____

_____

_____

_____

_____

_____

_____

_____

_____

_____

DAY 9

DEPRESSION

*"**Depression** begins with disappointment. When disappointment festers in our soul, it leads to discouragement."*

~ Joyce Meyer

DEPRESSION DEFINED: A sadness, inactivity, or difficulty in thinking and concentration; a significant increase or decrease in appetite and time spent sleeping; feeling of dejection and hopelessness, and sometimes suicidal tendencies.

Are you tired of being depressed? Tired of feeling this overwhelming sadness? My sister, my brother, you do not have to stay that way. Whether it's been a week, a few months or a few years I want to encourage you today, GOD IS ABLE! You must rehearse the good and be thankful for what God has already released in your life. In the midst of all you are facing, you can experience joy, peace, and contentment that comes from above. Our current circumstances should not dictate our emotions, we should always be governed by the words of our

Father. We must allow God's word to permeate our mind and our heart. I'm a witness that in **continual** communication and confession of His word, you will rise above it and the spirit of depression will lose its foothold. Shift your thought process, pray and believe. See yourself whole, alive and fruitful again, and it will be so.

Psalm 34:18
"If your heart is broken, you'll find GOD right there; if you're kicked in the gut, He'll help you catch your breath."

My Supplication: Lord, You are Emmanuel – God with us and I give You praise. I repent and ask forgiveness of my sins. Renew my walk with You and let me begin again. Thank You for never leaving or neglecting me. I'm crying.... H E L P!! My heart is so heavy, I'm broken in spirit. I need to feel Your presence here with me now. I'm so tired of life the way it is. Sometimes the pain is so great it takes my breath away. I feel as though I'm in an emotional prison and I want OUT. Father, please heal my fragmented heart now. Send Your loving angels to surround me like a shield and pick up the pieces of my brokenness. I want to be whole again. I trust in Your love for me, I trust You have great plans for me. Help me to take off this garment of heaviness and put on the garment of praise. Help me to think on things that are lovely, things that are of a good report to think on things that make me smile and confirms Your love for me. I lift up my voice right now and I praise You in the midst of my pain; I praise You for being my help, I praise You for being my deliverer, I praise You for healing my heart, I praise You for being my comforter. You are the lifter of my head and I say – THANK YOU. THANK YOU, JESUS, FOR YOUR HELP. Thank You now for Your love and power that's setting me free from the spirit of depression in Jesus' Name and by Your blood I pray Amen and Amen!

My Affirmation: I put a guard on my thoughts and think on things that only lift me up. I choose life, I choose joy, I choose peace. I choose to rest in God's care. Depression does not dominate me. My emotions are focused on God's goodness and love for me, therefore my spirit is lifted. Thank God I'm smiling again.

Meditation Scripture:

Philippians 4:8
"Finally, brethren, whatsoever things are true, whatsoever things are honest, whatsoever things are just, whatsoever things are pure, whatsoever things are lovely, whatsoever things are of good report; if there be any virtue, and if there be any praise, think on these things."

Application for the day:

_____

_____

_____

_____

_____

_____

_____

_____

_____

_____

_____

DAY 10

DETERMINATION

*"A dream doesn't become reality through magic; it takes sweat, **determination** and hard work."*

~ Colin Powell

DETERMINATION DEFINED: Firmness of purpose; resolution, resolve, willpower, strength of character, single-mindedness, purposefulness, intentness.

Who doesn't need this word in their life? Determination is simply refusing to give up, no matter how hard things get. All of us have something that we need to be determined and fixed on. I must confess in the midst of writing this book I was stuck for a time, clouded in my thoughts of inadequacy saying, *"it's just not good enough."* I almost used the "c" word, which I try to eliminate from my vocabulary because *I **CAN** DO ALL THINGS THROUGH CHRIST THAT STRENGTHENS ME.*

So, with purpose and a clear resolve, I'm determined to finish what I've started. We all have to embody determination in order to accomplish anything we put our hands to do, whether it's to write a book, open up a business, pass the bar, start a ministry etc. When you are in relationship with God, His power works through you and encourages you to be solid, stable and determined to never give up. We may not meet the mark each time but we should never quit or give up.

Numbers 13:30
"But Caleb calmed the congregation, and He spoke to Moses. We should go straight in, right away, and take it over.
We are surely able."

<u>My Supplication</u>: Great God, Great King – I give You honor this day. This is the day You have made I will rejoice and be glad in it. I confess my sins, known and unknown, asking Your help to make me better. Thank You for Your grace and all that You have done already. Father, I pray that You produce in me a mindset that is confident of the ability I have in You. <u>I realize that there will be a price for progress and with Your supervision I can say like Caleb *"I am surely able."*</u> Thank You for the spirit of determination. I will not be trapped and feel that I'm not capable of doing what I know You have given me to do. With Your help I will keep an attitude of confidence that will secure my

victory. Your word in Phil 1:6 says *"Being confident of this, that He who began a good work in ME will carry it on to completion until the day of Christ Jesus"*. Thank You for the strength to run after my destiny with great determination. I know that my assignment is greater than my attack and I will not allow it to slow me down. Because of a life-force of determination, I will rise to greater heights in You in Jesus' Name I pray – Amen!

My Affirmation: I AM DETERMNED TO NEVER GIVE UP! I will pay the price for progress and success – DETERMINATION. My greatest season is ahead of me. YAY!!! ☺

Meditation Scripture:

Deuteronomy 31:6
*"Be **determined** and confident. Do not be afraid of them. Your God, the Lord himself, will be with you. He will not fail you or abandon you."*

Application for the day:

_____

_____

_____

_____

_____

_____

_____

_____

_____

_____

_____

DAY 11

DISCIPLINE

*"Your **discipline** or lack of it is going to determine your destiny."*

~ Charles Stanley

DISCIPLINE DEFINED: The practice of training people to obey rules or a code of behavior.

One of my first and favorite teachings I ever heard from Joyce Meyer was a series given to me by Mother Joan Williams on DISCIPLINE. This teaching changed my life dramatically. Through this teaching I learned that discipline was more than just will power and praying: LORD HELP ME! Being disciplined was hard work. I was encouraged to start viewing discipline and self-control in a whole new way. I now view them as *helpful keys* to good health, peace, prosperity, better relationships, and the satisfaction of fulfilling Gods purpose in my life.

I've been disciplined for more than 10 years now in
the area of spending time with God daily. Now, it's
a part of my every day. No matter what, where or
how, I'm dedicated. I look forward to that time
with the Father and because of this discipline you
are reading this book today. ☺ So, I'm paying it
forward and I challenge you to take the discipline
challenge. For the remaining days, challenge
yourself to be disciplined to spend time with God
everyday be it morning, noon or night; just be
disciplined to make it happen **EVERY DAY**.
Prayerfully by the end of the challenge you would
have developed a healthy appetite for God's
presence.

Proverbs 23:12
*"Develop a **disciplined** life. Be attentive so you can
be well informed."*

<u>My Supplication</u>: I call You Marvelous, Majesty,
full of glory. How I worship You! I confess my sins
and I ask for Your forgiveness. Restore me, revive
me, I need You. Thank You for helping me develop
a disciplined life so I will be attentive and well
informed. Father I know that discipline is the
Godly way of living my life. I commit to listening to
needful criticism to acquire a better life. I know
I've missed the mark and have been lazy about my
relationship with You. I've put so many things and
people ahead of You for too long and I ask for Your
forgiveness. I take You at Your word and rely on

Your strength to help me change my ways. I know that with Your strength I can do all things. I'm willing to commit to my personal spiritual development by spending quality time with You on a daily basis. I will seek Your kingdom first and Your righteousness as You promised everything that's needed will be provided. I'm confident that embracing this way of living will open the door to new levels of maturity in You. Father, I draw on You, the master teacher, to teach me how to live a life of discipline so I may reach my highest potential. I'm thrilled to have You interceding on my behalf. I will press towards the mark for the prize of the high calling in You in the name of Jesus Christ I pray – Amen!

My Affirmation: I practice self-control. I do the right thing and make better choices to promote restraint to get to the finish line. I now possess positive, productive results from a disciplined life.

Meditation Scripture:

Proverbs 15:5
*"Only a fool despises a parent's **discipline**; whoever learns from correction is wise".*

Application for the day:

_____

_____

_____

_____

_____

_____

_____

_____

_____

_____

_____

DAY 12

DOUBT

*"**Doubt** discovers difficulties which it never solves; it creates hesitancy, despondency, despair. Its progress is the decay of comfort, the death of peace. "Believe!" is the word which speaks life into a man, but **doubt** nails down his coffin."*

~ Charles Spurgeon

DOUBT DEFINED: a feeling of uncertainty about the truth, reality, or nature of something; consider questionable or unlikely; hesitate to believe.

Some of us are just like doubting Thomas we can't believe it unless we see it. The scripture shares to not be faithless and incredulous, but stop your unbelief and believe. This should be our constant prayer; Lord help my unbelief.

Matthew 21:21
*"And Jesus answered them, Truly I say to you, if you have faith (a firm relying trust) and do not **doubt,** you will not only do what has been done to the fig tree, but even if you say to this mountain, Be taken up and cast into the sea, it will be done."*

My Supplication: Heavenly Father, you are the King of Kings and The Lord of Lords and I worship You. I come to You confessing my sin asking for forgiveness, I want to be near You. I thank You for eyes to see, ears to hear, legs to walk and a tongue to talk which I often take for granted. No doubt about it You have been faithful to me and I'm so grateful. Engrossed from the cares of life I have wavered from the firm relying trust I once had in You. You didn't answer in the manner I expected and I have doubted Your ability to come through. In spite of my doubts and fears Your faithfulness is still new every morning. I inquire of You Lord and I PRAY THIS DAY, HELP MY UNBELIEF! It is my desire to follow Your laws of faith and start anew. Please Father, help me do away with this doubtful bondage and infuse my life with faith to believe the impossible. Help me to be confident enough to speak with authority to the mountain of doubt to be removed and cast into the sea by the power of Your name and by Your blood. I pray this pray in faith in Jesus Name-Amen!

My Affirmation: I'm standing in my new liberation of faith that denounces all fear and doubt. According to Your word, *My mouth will be filled with Your wisdom that is wholehearted and straightforward, free for wavering and doubts.*
~ James 3:17

Meditation Scripture:

Psalm 86:2

*"Preserve my life, for I am godly and dedicated; O my God, save Your servant, for I trust in You [leaning and believing on You, committing all and confidently looking to You, without fear or **doubt**]."*

Application for the day:

_____

_____

_____

_____

_____

_____

_____

_____

_____

_____

_____

_____

DAY 13

FAITH

*"**Faith** sees the invisible, believes the unbelievable, and receives the impossible."*

~ Corrie Ten Boom

FAITH DEFINED: strong belief or trust in someone or something; belief in the existence of God: strong religious feelings or beliefs

Strong faith is one of the greatest defenses against hardships in life. As we make strides to focus on the source of our faith and not the source of our fears, we will blaze through the test of time. Keeping a prayer journal of all your past victories can aid in maintaining your trust and faith in God.

Do you know that without faith it is impossible to please God? In the bible, Abraham leads the way in demonstrating faith in God through his obedience. Bottom line, in order to accomplish anything in life we must believe that we can achieve it through the eyes of faith.

Hebrews 11:6
*"But without **faith** it is impossible to please him: for He that cometh to God must believe that He is, and that He is a rewarder of them that diligently seek him."*

<u>My Supplication</u>: Lord, you are my refuge my very present help in the time of trouble. I adore You and I give You continuous praise. I confess my iniquity to You and ask for forgiveness. I thank You for shining Your light of mercy upon me. I ask that You quiet my spirit to believe that You will take care of me. Eliminate all of the flaws in my faith that will unlock every door to the great future You have planned for me.

I thank You now for courage that fuels my faith every single day. I receive mountain moving faith, yes the faith that is the substance of things hope for and the evidence of things not seen, this is my prayer In Jesus Name— Amen!

<u>My Affirmation</u>: I will put my faith alongside my prayers and demonstrate my belief in God. My faith will be able to conquer anything. I CHOOSE TO WALK BY FAITH AND NOT BY SIGHT!

Meditation Scripture:

Hebrews 11:1-2
*"The fundamental fact of existence is that this trust in God, this **faith**, is the firm foundation under everything that makes life worth living. It's our handle on what we can't see. The act of faith is what distinguished our ancestors, set them above the crowd."*

Application for the day:

_____

_____

_____

_____

_____

_____

_____

_____

_____

_____

_____

DAY 14

FEAR

"The greatest mistake we make is living in constant fear that we will make one."

~ John C. Maxwell

FEAR DEFINED: An unpleasant emotion caused by the belief that someone or something is dangerous, likely to cause pain, or a threat.

Fear can also stand for: **F**alse **E**vidence **A**ppearing **R**eal. Fear is a liar and can be paralyzing. Fear will keep you from seeing the world, enjoying family and friends, pursuing a prospective relationship and landing that dream job. Don't lose your drive in the fear of *"what if's"*, when you can choose to believe God's best for your life. Being confident in who you are in Christ will help you face your fears head on. Praying prayers of faith will keep you standing tall no matter how unpleasant or threatening things may appear.

2 Timothy 1:7
"For God has not given us a spirit of fear, but of power and of love and of a sound mind."

My Supplication: My Heavenly Father, my protector in the time of distress, I love on You. I confess my sins and ask that You restore me to my rightful place in You. I thank You for the grace and mercy that follow me every day of my life and satisfy the longings of my heart. Father, I have lived in fear long enough and I ask that You grant me the strength needed to live a fearless life through an authentic relationship with You. I want to grab hold of the faith, power and love You have granted me in Your word. Thank You now for a sound mind to put things in perspective and get me on the right track.

It says in Your word that there is no fear in love and I desire to have the perfect love that casts out fear. By the power of the name of Jesus I release myself from every spirit of fear that has held me hostage. I now seize this day as a new beginning of a life full of freedom and enjoyment in Jesus' Name I pray – Amen!

My Affirmation: FEAR DOES NOT HAVE ME ANYMORE! I have the power, the love, and a sound mind that support my fearless life in Jesus Christ.

Meditation Scripture:

Isaiah 41:10

*"Fear not [there is nothing to **fear**], for I am with you; do not look around you in terror and be dismayed, for I am your God. I will strengthen and harden you to difficulties, yes, I will help you; yes, I will hold you up and retain you with My [victorious] right hand of rightness and justice."*

Application for the day:

_____

_____

_____

_____

_____

_____

_____

_____

_____

_____

_____

DAY 15

FORGIVENESS

"Forgiveness means accepting what is, and being willing to see it differently... It means letting go and not changing a single thing."

~ Iyanla Vanzant

FORGIVENESS DEFINED: the action or process of forgiving or being forgiven. Letting go of grudges and bitterness

Have you ever been in need of forgiveness? Well because we are not perfect beings at some point in life we all will need forgiveness. The next time you decide to dwell on unforgiveness I would like for you to ponder this: *Remember how it felt when you were pardoned and someone forgave you?* Can you be gracious enough to grant the same mercy to someone else? Forgiveness is liberating – JUST LET IT GO!

Matt. 18:21-22
*"Then Peter came to Jesus and asked, "Lord, how many times shall I **forgive** my brother or sister who sins against me? Up to seven times?" Jesus answered, "I tell you, not seven times, but seventy-seven times"*

My Supplication: Lord, You are faithful and true and the Father of mercies. Blessings be to Your name. I confess my sins and ask Your forgiveness. I thank You for being a faithful companion of love and acceptance. You delight in showing unfailing love. Only a wise God who forgives and pardons all of my guilt would welcome me back in His arms over and over again. I thank You for overlooking my sin and not staying angry with me forever. Your love continues to show me how I need to learn how to love and forgive others when they wrong me. Thank You for releasing me from resentment and self-righteousness. Just as You have repeatedly forgiven me I will humble myself and FORGIVE others, in Jesus Name I pray – Amen!

My Affirmation: FORGIVENESS IS MY CHOICE! No more grudges, No more bitterness. I let go, I move on, I make every day count. I will forgive as my Heavenly Father continues to forgive me. I look forward to the joy that forgiveness brings. (*Insert a smile right here. Yes – that would be you.) - LOL*

Meditation Scripture:

Mark 11:25
*"And when you stand praying, if you hold anything against anyone, **forgive** him, so that your Father in heaven may forgive you."*

Application for the day:

_____

_____

_____

_____

_____

_____

_____

_____

_____

_____

_____

_____

_____

DAY 16

GUIDANCE

"The BIBLE is our road map to a prosperous and holy life; when we get lost we can always find our way in God's word."

~ Nishan Panwar

GUIDANCE DEFINED: help or advice that tells you what to do; the act or process of guiding someone or something

The first principle in receiving God's guidance is knowing His word. Having the knowledge of God's word will direct your actions and decisions. It is written in Psalm 37:23 *"the steps of a good man are ordered by God and He delights in his way"*. Keep your heart fixed on following His way and trust the process.

Psalm 32:8
"I [the Lord] will instruct you and teach you in the way you should go; I will counsel you with My eye upon you."

My Supplication: Father with all my heart, I worship You and give You praise. You make my heart sing. I confess my sins for going ahead of You and doing my own thing. Thank You for never turning me away when I come back to You. Your concern for me lifts my spirits every time. I thank and praise You for being my guide, instructing me and teaching me in the way I should go. Thank You for Your wise counsel and keeping an eye on me. You lead me in all truth and I am so grateful.

When I wait on Your direction You keep my steps firm and on a straight path. As I acknowledge You in all my ways You assured me You would direct my path and this time....I'm going to let You do that. I'm confident I will not falter as I depend on Your guidance for all my endeavors. I appreciate You, it is in Your powerful name **Jesus** that I share this prayer – **A**...men!

My Affirmation: Today, I purpose to no longer walk aimlessly through life wondering what will be my next step. I'm doing the word and I'm seeking God's guidance and gaining wisdom every step of the way.

Meditation Scripture:

Isaiah 58:11
"And the Lord shall guide you continually and satisfy you in drought and in dry places and make strong your bones. And you shall be like a watered garden and like a spring of water whose waters fail not."

Application for the day:

_____

_____

_____

_____

_____

_____

_____

_____

_____

_____

_____

_____

DAY 17

HEALING

"Christ is the Good Physician. There is no disease He cannot heal; no sin He cannot remove; no trouble He cannot help. He is the Balm of Gilead, the Great Physician who has never yet failed to heal all the spiritual maladies of every soul that has come unto Him in faith and prayer."

~ **James H. Aughey**

HEALING DEFINED: The process of making or becoming sound or healthy again; to ease or relieve, to set right, repair; to recover from an illness or injury; return to health.

During my journey through Cancer I quoted this daily. Read it out loud...

"The healing power of God is working in me right now. Every day I get better and better in every way."
~ **Joyce Meyer**

My mouth was filled with God's promises on healing every day. I encourage you to do the same.

If you are in need of a healing – **GOD IS A HEALER!** God does not have a respect of persons but He does have a respect of faith. If you have faith as a mustard seed you will have the power to speak to mountains and they will be removed. The word says that NOTHING WILL BE IMPOSSIBLE FOR THOSE THAT BELIEVE. If you can only believe, healing is yours. According to your faith, be it unto you. Healing _is_ the children's bread. God delights in our prosperity, not only physically but mentally, spiritually and emotionally. He wants us to be free and prayer is the vehicle to get you to wholeness. Let us draw upon the wealth of God's grace to withstand this journey of faith. Live in prayer and you will not only know him as healer you will know him as friend.

Psalm 103:1-5
*"Bless the LORD, O my soul; And all that is within me, bless His holy name. Bless the LORD, O my soul, And forget not all His benefits: Who forgives all your iniquities, Who **heals** all your diseases, Who redeems your life from destruction, Who crowns you with loving kindness and tender mercies, Who satisfies your mouth with good things, So that your youth is renewed like the eagle's."*

My Supplication: Gracious Father, I praise You and exalt Your name for it is because of You that l live, move and have my being. Thank You for forgiving my sins and healing my disease. I praise You for redeeming my life from destruction and crowning me with Your loving kindness and tender mercies. Thank You for dismantling every spirit of darkness that would try to delay my promise of healing and restoration. I'm leaping for joy that You satisfy my mouth with good things and renew my strength like the eagle's. Father, forgive me for being skeptical about Your ability to heal me and make me whole again. It is written in Your word that a merry heart is as good as a medicine so I thank You now for a merry heart. My merry heart brings a smile to my face and lifts my countenance.

I feel Your presence right now doing the inside job that's needed. I praise You in advance for the completed work. You promised to daily load me with benefits and I receive the benefit of Your healing power working in me right now in Jesus' Name I pray – Amen!

My Affirmation: The life of God is permeating in my body, bringing health and wholeness to all my being. The weapon of sickness and disease shall NOT prosper in my body, for my body is the temple of God.

I FURTHER AFFIRM ACCORDING TO GOD'S WORD:

~ I AM HEALED BY HIS STRIPES (Isa.53:5)

~ I AM REDEEMED FROM SICKNESS AND DISEASE (Gal. 3:13)

~ I PROSPER AND WALK IN HEALTH EVEN AS MY SOUL PROSPSERS (3 JOHN 2)

~ I CRIED UNTO THE LORD AND HE HAVE HEALED ME (Psa. 30:2)

~ I SHALL NOT DIE BUT LIVE TO DECLARE THE WORKS OF THE LORD (Psa.118:17)

~ THE LORD WILL RESTORE ME TO HEALTH AND HEAL MY WOUNDS (Jer.30:17)

~ THE LORD FORGIVES ALL OF MY SINS AND HEALS MY DISEASES (Psa.103:3)

~ THE LORD HEALS MY BROKEN HEART AND BINDS UP MY WOUNDS (Psa.147:3)

~ EVERY ORGAN IN MY BODY FUNCTIONS THE WAY GOD INTENDED (Psa.139:1)

~ JESUS CHRIST MAKES ME WHOLE (Acts 9:34)

HALLELUJAH – I AM HEALED!

Meditation Scriptures:

Jeremiah 17: 14
"Heal me, O Lord, and I shall be healed; save me, and I shall be saved, for You are my praise."

Prov. 17:22
"A merry heart doeth good like a medicine; but a broken spirit drieth the bones."

Psalm 118:17
"I shall not die, but live, and declare the works of the LORD."

Application for the day:

_____

_____

_____

_____

_____

_____

_____

_____

_____

_____

_____

DAY 18

INTEGRITY

"Be Impeccable With Your Word. Speak with integrity. Say only what you mean. Avoid using the word to speak against yourself or to gossip about others. Use the power of your word in the direction of truth and love."

~ **Miguel Ruiz**

INTEGRITY DEFINED: firm adherence to a code of especially moral or artistic values; incorruptibility; an unimpaired condition; soundness, the quality or state of being complete or undivided; completeness.

Powerful word! Oh what joy comes from doing the right thing, especially when no one is looking (*eye brow raised*). That's integrity, being honest and true to oneself and others. It's a lifelong achievement for us all. Let us determine to be women/men of our word. A person that is reliable and full of wholeness.

Proverbs 10:9
*"Whoever walks in **integrity** walks securely, but He who makes his ways crooked will be found out."*

<u>**My Supplication:**</u> Father I give you glory, honor and praise. I am grateful for Your continued forgiveness for my short comings. Thank You for always coming through for me. I appreciate Your dedication to ironing out every detail of my life. With Your grace I will securely walk in integrity and refrain from crooked ways.

Thank You for a sure foundation and wholeness in You. I will not be divided, I will represent You with sincerity of heart and soundness of mind. It's because of You I can walk boldly performing good works. As Your servant I will continually seek Your road map for all future endeavors to bring glory to Your name, in Jesus Name I pray – Amen!

<u>**My Affirmation:**</u> Integrity is my name. I will be partners with kindness and truth, never to let them leave me. I find favor in the sight of God and man because, I AM INTEGRITY!

Meditation Scripture:

Titus 2:7-8

"Show yourself in all respects to be a model of good works, and in your teaching show integrity, dignity, and sound speech that cannot be condemned, so that an opponent may be put to shame, having nothing evil to say about us."

Application for the day:

_____

_____

_____

_____

_____

_____

_____

_____

_____

_____

_____

_____

DAY 19

LOVE

*"The best use of life is **love**. The best expression of **love** is time. The best time to **love** is now."*

~ **Rick Warren**

LOVE DEFINED: a profoundly tender, passionate affection for another person. A feeling of warm personal attachment or deep affection, as for a parent, child, or friend.

Love is an action word. Everyone I know wants to be loved and receive love. God the author of love shows us profoundly His *"unconditional love"* for us. The scriptures are very clear on how God's love for us was put in action John 3:16: *"For God so loved the word that He gave his only begotten son"*. He created this world for us, He died for us, He chose us and He cares for us – that's love.

1 Corinthians 13:4-8b
"Love is patient, love is kind. It does not envy, it does not boast, it is not proud. It does not dishonor others, it is not self-seeking, it is not easily angered, it keeps no record of wrongs. Love does not delight in evil but rejoices with the truth. It always protects, always trusts, always hopes, always perseveres. **Love never fails.***"*

<u>My Supplication</u>: Father, You are love, You are life, You are Lord of All and I sing praises to Your name. I confess my sins and say: sorry for not walking in love like I know I should. Your ongoing forgiveness warms my heart. Thank You for Your indescribable gift. Lord I love You, I ask....teach me how.... Teach me how to *<u>really</u>* love You. I want to walk in love. I'm talking about that unconditional love that You grant me each day. Teach me how to give that away. Teach me to obey Your word and forgive others and to love my neighbors as I love myself. Wait – first, I need to learn how to love me. I can't give away something that I don't have myself. So...today, I receive Your love for myself first so I can love others just as You have loved me.

As I receive Your love I receive patience and the love that displays kindness, Your love that's never envious, nor boastful or full of pride. It's the love that does not dishonor others and is definitely not self –seeking. Yes, it's the love that is not easily angered or offended, it's the God kind of love that keeps no record of wrong. The love that doesn't delight in evil but rejoices with the truth. Thank You Daddy, for giving me the love that protects, always trust, always hopes and always perseveres and the love that never fails. Thank You **Father I'm walking in love and it feels so good. This is my prayer in Jesus Name, it is so – thanks for listening, Amen.**

My Affirmation: Today, I celebrate the power of God's love for me. I'm empowered to love others unconditionally. I welcome God's love in my heart; come make a home in me. I will make a conscious effort to not just say *"I love you"* but, show that I LOVE YOU!

Meditation Scripture:

Matthew 22:37-39
"Jesus replied: 'Love the Lord your God with all your heart and with all your soul and with all your mind.' This is the first and greatest commandment. And the second is like it: 'Love your neighbor as yourself'."

Application for the day:

_____

_____

_____

_____

_____

_____

_____

_____

_____

_____

_____

DAY 20

OBEDIENCE

*"**Obedience** to God is the pathway to the life you really want to live".*

~ Joyce Meyer

OBEDIENCE DEFINED: compliance with an order, request, or law or submission to another's authority.

Obedience is hearing the voice of God and governing ourselves accordingly. John 14:23 Jesus replied: *if anyone loves me, He will obey my teachings. My Father will love him and we will come to him and make our home with him.* I don't know about you but I want the Father to come and make a home with me. A desire to obey the will of God is motivated in prayer. By being obedient, we secure God's blessings and gain spiritual insight. A life of obedience to God, is a rewarding life.

Psalm 91:11
*"For He will give His angels [especial] charge over you to accompany and defend and preserve you in all your ways [of **obedience** and service]."*

<u>My Supplication</u>: Father, You are the King of Glory, Lord strong and mighty. I'm singing Your praises from the mountaintop, You are miraculous. Thank You for forgiving me of my sins and repairing my relationship with You. Have mercy on me. I ask that You take away every defiant spirit that hinders my compliance to Your words. Thank You for giving Your angels charge over me to defend and preserve me in all my ways of obedience and service to You. As I obey Your words, I know You will replace sadness with joy, defeat to victory and weariness to praise. I'm ready to experience the joy of obeying Your directives. I respectfully submit to what You require of me in Jesus Name – Amen!

<u>My Affirmation</u>: I will turn to God with my heart and soul and reverently adhere to His words. My deeds and actions will back up my commitment to walk in obedience to Him.

Meditation Scripture:

Deuteronomy 13:4
*"You shall walk after the Lord your God and [reverently] fear Him, and keep His commandments and **obey** His voice, and you shall serve Him and cling to Him."*

Application for the day:

_____

_____

_____

_____

_____

_____

_____

_____

_____

_____

_____

_____

DAY 21

PATIENCE

"Patience is not the ability to wait but the ability to keep a good attitude while waiting."

~ Joyce Meyer

PATIENCE DEFINED: The quality of being patient, as the bearing of provocation; an ability or willingness to suppress restlessness or annoyance when confronted with delay.

I know you don't want to hear it but (*read this slowly*), **Patience is polished in tough times.** When you're frustrated with the waiting process and act outside of God's will, you ruin things for yourself. SLOW DOWN AND BE PATIENT. Always seek God's wisdom, and follow His instructions. Keep in mind that *"those who wait on the Lord will increase in strength"*. Isaiah 40:31

Psalm 40:1
"I waited patiently and expectantly for the Lord;
and He inclined to me and heard my cry."

My Supplication: Righteous Father, You are the ultimate gift. I love and adore You. I ask for Your forgiveness for not being patient. Thank You for Your compassion towards me. I need to rush and say thank You for Your patience with me. You continue to pardon me over and over again. Teach me how to be patient with others as You are patient with me. As You incline Your ear to me, teach me how to wait patiently and wait with expectancy for God's finest. Father please help me to wait with the right attitude. I know that Your timing is the best for me and I want to be in the center of Your will so please favor me, hear my call for help. I take my hands off and allow You to fix it and fix me in Jesus Name I pray – Amen!

My Affirmation: I demonstrate patience with the correct attitude today. As I recall God's never-ending patience and forgiveness for me, I lavish my consideration on others. I wait patiently and reap benefits of wide open doors of opportunity as I reflect the image of the God I serve.

Meditation Scripture:

Colossians 1:11

*"[We pray] that you may be invigorated and strengthened with all power according to the might of His glory, [to exercise] every kind of endurance and **patience** (perseverance and forbearance) with joy."*

Application for the day:

_____

_____

_____

_____

_____

_____

_____

_____

_____

_____

_____

_____

DAY 22

PEACE

"Peace is the deliberate adjustment of my life to the will of God."

~ Anonymous

PEACE DEFINED: A state in which there is no war or fighting. Freedom from disturbance; quiet and tranquility.

Peace can be called God's encouraging gift. It's the knowing He is with you, no matter what happens in life. I have experienced that special gift time and time again. Any individual that has God's genuine peace can experience an earthquake in their life and still have inner peace. It is my belief that only with an intimate relationship with God you can confidently live in PEACE.

Psalm 29:11
*"The LORD gives strength to his people: the LORD blesses his people with **peace**."*

My Supplication: Father, you are my shield, my protection and peace. I confess my sins to You and I thank You for wiping them all away. I thank You for delivering my soul in peace from the battle that is against me. You said in Your word that You would give me strength and bless me with peace.

As I keep my mind stayed on You, I can expect perfect peace, relying and trusting in You. I'm starting to understand that as I strengthen my relationship with You my peace will be strengthened also. Lord, I ask You, show me Your favor with the spirit of peace that I will be able to share the same peace with others, in Jesus Name- Amen!

My Affirmation: Regardless of the environment in which I live today, I believe and I receive God's peace. I hug His peace always, *by all means, for all times.* The peace that I have in God continues to surpass **MY** understanding.

Meditation Scripture:

John 14:27
*"I am leaving you with a gift—**peace** of mind and heart. And the **peace** I give is a gift the world cannot give. So don't be troubled or afraid."*

Application for the day:

_____

_____

_____

_____

_____

_____

_____

_____

_____

_____

_____

_____

_____

DAY 23

PROTECTION

"Now, this is what the Lord says, 'Fear not, for I have redeemed you; I have summoned you by name; you are mine. When you pass through the waters, I will be with you; and when you pass through the rivers, they will not sweep over you. When you walk through the fire, you will not be burned; the flames will not set you ablaze. For I am the Lord, your God, the Holy One of Israel, your Savior'."

~ Isaiah 43:1-3

PROTECTION DEFINED: The act of protecting, defense shelter from evil preservation from loss, injury or annoyance.

Psalm 91 tells us there's no safer place than in the center of Gods will. It says, *"He will cover you with his feathers, and under his wings you will find refuge; his faithfulness will be your shield and rampart".*

A danger free environment is not promised but you can be assured God will provide a refuge for those who love Him.

Psalm 5:12
*"LORD, when You bless good people, You surround them with Your love, like a large shield that **protects** them."*

<u>My Supplication</u>: Heavenly Father, You are My God and Your Word is True. I stand in awe of Your greatest. You are a Strong Tower where I can run in and be safe. I confess my sins to You and ask for Your forgiveness. Thank You for Your preserving power. Your existence is like a large shield of **protection** that surrounds me everywhere I go. You have set angels in place to guard over me. I lift my voice in praise saying: PRAISE BE TO GOD WHO HAS PROTECTED ME FROM THE HAND OF THE ENEMY. I dwell in quiet resting places because of You. I give You a heartfelt *"thank You"* for never being too busy to hear and help. My mouth is filled with gratitude, You're the best bodyguard ever. *I love You.* In Jesus Name I pray – Amen!

My Affirmation: Because I am *protected* by God my enemies will not triumph over me. I have angels on assignment to watch over me. Singing......Safe In His Arms. ☺

Meditation Scripture:

2 Thessalonians 3:3
" But the Lord can be trusted to make you strong and protect you from harm."

Application for the day:

_____

_____

_____

_____

_____

_____

_____

_____

_____

_____

_____

_____

_____

DAY 24

PROVISION

"The size of a challenge should never be measured by what we have to offer. It will never be enough. Furthermore, provision is God's responsibility, not ours. We are merely called to commit what we have - even if it's no more than a sack lunch."

~ Charles R. Swindoll

PROVISION DEFINED: The act or process of supplying or providing something; something that is done in advance to prepare for something else.

My prayer is that we would learn to view God's provision differently. Waking up each morning is God's provision. God provides life each day; clothes to wear, food to eat, a place to sleep, and the list goes on. Not once have I been in want and God hasn't provided. God delights in providing our requests. His provisions for us are endless. Trust God to provide whatever is needed, don't limit his capability to blow your mind at any time. See things *differently.*

Psalm 111:5
*"He has given food and **provision** to those who*
reverently and worshipfully fear Him; He will
remember His covenant forever and imprint it [on
His mind]."

My Supplication: Lord, You are Jehovah-Jireh my provider. I give You glory, honor and praise. You are my source and my *resource*. I thank You for your grace and all You have done. I repent of my sins and I ask for Your forgiveness. Thank You for keeping Your covenant and providing for me forever. You amaze me with Your abundant provision continually. I come asking You to provide once again. I believe Your desire for me is to prosper even as my soul prospers and today I desire provision for my SOUL, BODY AND SPIRIT. I pray that You will endow me with the ability to hear Your voice *clearly* and obey Your voice *immediately*. I stand in great expectation of Your word ministering life to my whole being. In Jesus' Name, I'm praising You in advance – Amen!

My Affirmation: I have unlimited resources available to me because of my relationship with my Heavenly Father. He grants me everything I need. I never worry about anything!

Meditation Scripture:

Genesis 22:14

*"Abraham called the name of that place The LORD Will Provide, as it is said to this day, "In the mount of the LORD it will be **provided**."*

Application for the day:

_____

_____

_____

_____

_____

_____

_____

_____

_____

_____

_____

_____

DAY 25

PURPOSE

*"You cannot fulfill God's **purposes** for your life while focusing on your own plans."*

~ Rick Warren

PURPOSE DEFINED: The reason for which something is done or created, or for which something exists.

Do you believe that everyone is born with a purpose? I mean a reason for which we were created? I do, and knowing that purpose gives us the fortitude to use our gifts and talents to enhance our lives and bring fulfillment. We should purposefully live to impact the lives around us to create positive change in our world. By doing so, we will be demonstrating the characteristics of our Father and living a life of purpose.

Ephesians 3:20
*"Now to Him Who, by (in consequence of) the [action of His] power that is at work within us, is able to [carry out His **purpose** and] do superabundantly, far over and above all that we [dare] ask or think*

[infinitely beyond our highest prayers, desires, thoughts, hopes, or dreams]."

My Supplication: Lord, I give You glory that is due to Your name. Wonderful Savoir You are. I confess my sins and ask for Your forgiveness. Thank You for Your continued goodness toward me. Father, sometimes it's hard to understand Your purpose for my life but I choose to believe that You are at work within me. I seek Your face, I know You have plans to prosper me and not to harm me, plans to give me hope and a future. I need You to reveal Your plan for my life. I want to reach my fullest potential and leave this earth empty. I praise You for carrying out Your purpose in me, for doing far more than I could ever imagine and even dare to ask or think. Help me to push past my problems, learn to grow from them and use them on purpose to lift others. Thank You now for guiding me, directing me and filling me with Your understanding to see things from Your perspective from this day forward In Jesus' Name I pray – Amen!

My Affirmation: I am a purpose driven individual. I live life on purpose, taking steps towards each goal to maximize every moment. I use my life and pursue my passion purposefully.

Meditation Scripture:

Proverbs 4: 25
*"Let your eyes look right on [with fixed **purpose**], and let your gaze be straight before you."*

Application for the day:

_____

_____

_____

_____

_____

_____

_____

_____

_____

_____

_____

_____

DAY 26

REJECTION

"Rejection doesn't mean you are not good enough;
it means the other person failed to notice what
you have to offer."
~ **Mark Amend**

REJECTION DEFINED: The act of rejecting or
state of being rejected. The bible speaks of how
Jesus was despised and rejected by man. If you
have ever experienced rejection, you know that it
can be depleting. Our Savior, the giver of life, can
bring healing and restoration. He is sympathetic to
our common feelings of rejection. If we draw near
to God, we can find the comfort that we need, even
in the midst of feeling rejected and abandoned. It
was God's compassionate love, the power of prayer,
and the confession of his words that rescued me
from a very dark place that I care never to visit
again!

Just know that GOD is always willing and ready to
heal your hurt that has been caused by rejection.
You can be assured that He values and validates
you as the Apple of His Eye.

Leviticus 26:11
*"I will set My dwelling in and among you, and My soul shall not despise or **reject** or separate itself from you."*

My Supplication: My Father, You are my friend and my consolation. How can I ever repay You? My obedience is my worship. I thank You for loving me. Your love gives me the fuel to drive full speed ahead when I feel like I'm empty. I confess my sins to You and ask for Your forgiveness. Thanks to You, I can say I'm a proud recipient of Your extravagant grace. I have often felt rejected, abandoned and left out by people. You, oh God, stick to me just like glue, closer than a brother. You have picked me up out of a horrible pit of rejection. No matter who's against me, I'm confident of Your loyalty to be right by my side. I have no need to fret or fear. Your love validates me and approves me. I can say in a loud voice: **I MATTER TO GOD!!** I matter to God. My heart is lifted and my spirit is revived this is my prayer and praise in Jesus' Name I pray – Amen!

My Affirmation: I am not a cast away, I am beloved by God. Before anybody can reject me, He already loves me. I have compassion and protection by Him. I GIVE HIM PRAISE!

Meditation Scripture:

Psalm 27:10
"Even if my father and mother abandon me,
the LORD will hold me close."

Application for the day:

_____

_____

_____

_____

_____

_____

_____

_____

_____

_____

_____

_____

_____

DAY 27

STRENGTH

*"Praying daily helps you attain **strength** to cross every red sea in your life."*

~ Arlene Mitchell

STRENTH DEFINED: the quality or state of being strong, mental power, force, or vigor.

After losing my job when I just moved into my new place it was God's strength that gave me that overcoming power to stand on His promise of provision for me. Because of God's past record of honoring His word I had the strength to stand in faith to believe that He would hear my cry for help once again. Indeed He is my refuge and strength, very present help in the time of trouble.

Philippians 4:13
*"I have **strength** for all things in Christ Who empowers me [I am ready for anything and equal to anything through Him Who infuses inner strength into me; I am self-sufficient in Christ's sufficiency]."*

My Supplication: My faithful God, I adore You and bless Your Holy name. I ask that You forgive my sin and give me another chance to make things right. Thank You for Your unending love and grace that continues to bless me daily. Father, Your word says that I have strength for all things and that You will empower me to be ready to handle anything. I receive that strength now. I thank You for infusing inner strength in me with Your abundance. My flesh and my heart may fail, but God You are my Rock and firm Strength, You are my portion forever. I relax in Your strength to see me through. It's amazing to know that Your strength is made perfect in my weaknesses, THANK YOU JESUS Amen and Amen.

My Affirmation: Because You are my *strength* I will not cave in during circumstances that seem beyond my comprehension. I will be strong as a mountain and trust in Your sovereignty.

Meditation Scripture:

Psalm 18:1-2
"I love You, LORD,   You are my **strength**. *The LORD is my rock, my fortress, and my savior; my God is my rock, in whom I find protection. He is my shield, the power that saves me, and my place of safety."*

Application for the day:

_____

_____

_____

_____

_____

_____

_____

_____

_____

_____

_____

_____

DAY 28

THANKFULNESS

*"Be **thankful** for what you have; you'll end up having more. If you concentrate on what you don't have, you will never, ever have enough."*

~ **Oprah Winfrey**

THANKFULNESS DEFINED: Aware and appreciative of a benefit; grateful. Expressive of gratitude: *(insert a thankful smile.)* ☺

Understanding the power of THANKFULNESS has shaped my world into something more beautiful than I ever imagined. After hearing a dear friend, Evangelist Betty Lawrence, praying *"Before I ask You for anything I want to thank You for everything,"* I immediately incorporated that into my daily devotion to God. Each day, I wake saying: "THANK YOU." A prayer of thanksgiving is my favorite prayer to pray, because I always want to be thankful for all that God has done ALREADY. Sometimes we tend to focus on asking, asking and asking some more. How about just saying: THANK YOU. I pray that you will see the need to invite "THANKFULNESS" into your sphere. I can guarantee, you will experience less stress, more joy, more appreciation, and more smiles just to name a few. Our thankfulness develops an appreciative heart and compassion for others. Having a relationship with thankfulness allows us to rise above troubled times that can bring on depression. Thankfulness leaves us empowered and full of gratefulness, so be encouraged to take on the spirit of thankfulness today.

1 Thessalonians 5:18
"Thank [God] in everything [no matter what the circumstances may be, be thankful and give thanks], for this is the will of God for you [who are] in Christ Jesus [the Revealer and Mediator of that will]."

<u>**My Supplication:**</u> Lord, You are the center of my joy. You are my El Shaddai – more than enough. I repent and ask for forgiveness for anything I have done against Your will. I'm so thankful for all You have done. Father, if I had 10,000 tongues, I couldn't say thank You enough for creating me in Your image and calling me "beloved." You are great and greatly to be praised, and You are worthy of a thousand HALLELUJAH'S. I honor You and thank You for not once getting tired of blessing me and listening to my prayers. Lord, I thank You for never changing, for You are the same yesterday, today and forever more. You are always providing for me, protecting me, guiding me, opening doors for me, delivering me, healing me, sustaining me, being

faithful to me and genuinely loving me for the person I am. My heart is jam-packed with praise and adoration for all You have done for me and my family. I offer my thanks to You and I let go of the cares of this world, I trust You and I will rest in Your Sovereignty. I will obey Your words and be thankful always in everything. Just like the one leper who came back to say thanks, I say thank You for healing me, Father. I will never forget Your faithfulness. I go as far to say I VOW to always have a spirit of thankfulness. This is my heartfelt prayer in Jesus' Name– Amen!

My Affirmation: I will never forget Your labor of love towards me. THANKFULNESS will be my dwelling place. You have gone above and beyond demonstrating Your unconditional love and care for me all my days. I'm indebted to You, Father. My heart says: THANK YOU!

Meditation Scripture:

2 Corinthians 9:15
*"Now **thanks** be to God for His Gift, [precious] beyond telling [His indescribable, inexpressible, free Gift]"*

Application for the day:

_____

_____

_____

_____

_____

_____

_____

_____

_____

_____

_____

_____

DAY 29

TRUST

*"We **trust** as we love, and where we love. If we love Christ much, surely we shall trust him much."*

~ Thomas Brooks

TRUST DEFINED: Firm belief in the reliability, truth, ability, or strength of someone or something.

I would like to invite you to have a firm belief and reliance in God's word. Trusting God is nurtured in daily devotion and spending time in His presence. When you are fully aware of His love for you and committed to trust God you become unshakeable. If you consistently rely on His ability to produce what He promises, trusting Him becomes the standard of living.

Psalm 37:3
*"**Trust** (lean on, rely on, and be confident) in the Lord and do good; so shall you dwell in the land and feed surely on His faithfulness, and truly you shall be fed."*

My Supplication: Father, I adore You for You are Jehovah-Jirah my God that provides. I confess my sin and ask for Your forgiveness. Dismiss all distractions that would disrupt my connection with You. I thank You for all of the benefits that You load me with daily. My desire is to TRUST, lean on and be confident in You. I want to do good and dwell in You and feed on Your faithfulness. I'm certain that as I trust You I will be led into a new land of stillness and rest that is beyond my intellectual capacity. May my confidence in You never be shaken as I study Your words and become acquainted with Your power. I pray Isaiah 26:4, *"I will trust in You Lord I will commit myself to You and lean to You, hope confidently in You forever; for You oh lord is my everlasting rock.* In Jesus Name I pray – Amen!

My Affirmation: My mind is set! I will not allow contrary situations to move me from my trust in God's ability. I know that Gods word is accurate and I will be motionless with my trust in HIM!

Meditation Scripture:

Proverbs 3:5-6
"Trust in the Lord with all your heart and lean not on your own understanding; in all your ways acknowledge him, and He shall direct your paths."

Application for the day:

_____

_____

_____

_____

_____

_____

_____

_____

_____

_____

_____

_____

_____

_____

DAY 30

WISDOM

"What you read between the covers of your Bible is **wisdom** *for a lifetime, rock-solid, forever truth— truth you can stand on, live by, and trust...forever."*

~ Elizabeth George

WISDOM DEFINED: The quality or state of being wise; knowledge of what is true or right coupled with just judgment as to action; sagacity, discernment, or insight.

Prayer is the primary ingredient to obtaining the wisdom of God. We pray to attain God's wisdom, but we are also required to continually seek, surrender to and act upon His will. God promises to give wisdom to us in abundance, if we would just ask. I have chosen to make wisdom my close relative. I call her my sister.

With wisdom we are able to make wise decisions and offer significant contributions to all of the lives that surround us. You see, having God's wisdom equips us to handle life as it really is.

James 1:5
*"But if any of you lacks **wisdom**, let him ask of God, who gives to all generously and without reproach, and it will be given to him."*

My Supplication: My Father, My King. I worship You. You are my source for everything. Thank You for forgiving me of my sins and restoring me to my rightful place in You. I know I lack wisdom and I humbly ask that You generously endow me with Your wisdom and guide me along the correct path. You said in Your word that from Your mouth comes knowledge and understanding, and today, I embrace all aspects of them as I walk in obedience before You. Thank You now for shielding me as I walk with integrity to do Your will. I praise You for Your divine insight as I strive to be faithful to You in all that I do, in Jesus' Name – Amen!

My Affirmation: I have the mind of Christ and I conduct my life with God's wisdom. I make wise decisions that keep my life aligned with His word. I continually seek His wisdom to set the boundaries needed to live more wisely.

Meditation Scripture:

Proverbs 2:6-8
*"For the LORD grants **wisdom!** From his mouth
come knowledge and understanding.
He grants a treasure of common sense to the
honest. He is a shield to those who walk with
integrity. He guards the paths of the just and
protects those who are faithful to him."*

Application for the day:

_____

_____

_____

_____

_____

_____

_____

_____

_____

_____

_____

_____

CONGRATULATIONS

YOU DID IT!! I'm so proud of you. ☺

You have just completed Prayer - The Lifestyle, A 30 day prayer challenge to a better relationship with God.

If you have dedicated 30 consecutive days to:

- Praying Scripture prayers
- Declaring the daily affirmations
- Meditating on God's word
- Writing down your application for the day

I am confident your relationship with God has been made better.

So you may ask.....what now?

Start over again, read it – re-read it, then read it again.

Zig Ziglar says often: "*Repetition is the mother of all learning*". The more you get familiar with reading God's word and communicating with God in prayer on a daily basis, I can guarantee that your perception on your life challenges will significantly change.   My prayer for you is that you will continue using this powerful resource called PRAYER and soar into victorious living in Christ Jesus.

If this book has been a blessing to you, be a blessing to someone else. Prayerfully consider purchasing it for someone in need of prayer.

I would love to hear from you. Please take the time to share your Prayer – The Lifestyle 30 day challenge experiences with me.

Feel free to leave me a message at:
www.arlenemitchell.com

Well....until the next book....

In the words of my father in the gospel Arch Bishop Roy. E. Brown, as I often quote:

I LOVE YOU AND THERE IS NOTHING YOU CAN DO ABOUT IT! ☺

INVITATION

A SPECIAL INVITATION JUST FOR YOU

For those of you that may be reading this book and do not have a personal relationship with Christ, I want to extend a "life transforming" invitation to begin a relationship with Him today.

Romans 10:9-10 (New Living Translation)
If you openly declare that Jesus is Lord and believe in your heart that God raised him from the dead, you will be saved.

For it is by believing in your heart that you are made right with God, and it is by openly declaring your faith that you are saved.

So, I invite you to accept the Lord's invitation to be a part of His family by saying this prayer:

Sinner's Prayer
Lord Jesus, I am a sinner. I ask you to forgive me, save me, live in me. I believe that you died and you rose again just for me. I now accept you in my heart as my personal Savior and Lord of my life. In Jesus Name - I AM SAVED - AMEN!

REFERENCES

I want to acknowledge and thank the following for making their information available for my use:

Ministries:
Joyce Meyer Ministries
In Touch Ministries
Revive Our Hearts
Christian's Handbook, Pilgrim & Scripture Church

Dictionaries:
The Free Dictionary
Webster Merriam
Dictionary.com
King James Dictionary

Resources (On and off-line):
BIBLEGATEWAY.COM
Bible Hub
Good Reads
Inspirational Verses
www.edpaul.us/peace
FREE BIBLE STUDY GUIDE

BIBLE VERSIONS USED:
The Message (MSG)
The Amplified (AMP)
International Standard version (ISV)
Century Eastern Version (CEV)
New living Translation (NLT)
Good News Translation (GNT)
King James Version (KJV)

ABOUT THE AUTHOR

Through her passion to empower others, Minister Arlene Mitchell renders community service by visiting Shelters and Nursing Homes to share her gift of song and encouragement through the word of God. She also conducts weekly prayer conference calls that support Cancer Patients/Caregivers and people in need of encouragement. Reports have been given of healing, deliverance, restoration, and salvation giving all glory and honor to God. She is humbled and grateful to be the CANCERFREE visionary of *Arlene Mitchell Ministries* which includes several ministries of prayer that maintain the commission the Lord gave her mother over 40 years ago. A ministry which focuses on ministering to hurting people and equipping them through the power of prayer and the word of God to face life challenges. She also hosts an annual event called "The Sister Saturday Experience" that celebrates and educates women of their worth to GOD and the necessity of true Sisterhood. It has received numerous reports being a "life changing experience".

She has recently expanded the ministry to include an annual Men's Empowerment Forum to inspire and promote effective Godly leadership among men. Minister Mitchell exuberantly cheers of her survival of Breast Cancer not once, but TWICE. She indeed is an overcomer and a "MIRACLE IN MOTION"! Her heart's desire is to impact the lives of everyone she comes in contact with by sharing the miracle working power that God has performed in her life. She endeavors to let the Word of God dwell in her richly as she ministers with a grateful heart for a second chance at LIFE.

For assistance in cultivating a life style of prayer, Minister Mitchell offers (one on one) Personal Prayer Coaching and invites you to participate in her ministries. For more information, you can contact her at:

Email: Admin@arlenemitchell.com
Website: www.arlenemitchell.com
Facebook: Arlene Mitchell
Twitter: ArleneMIM